Big Five
of Africa

Big Five
of Africa

GERALD HINDE

Struik Nature
(an imprint of Penguin Random House (Pty) Ltd)
Reg. No. 1953/000441/07
The Estuaries No. 4, Oxbow Crescent,
Century Avenue, Century City
PO Box 1144, Cape Town, 8000 South Africa

Visit **www.randomstruik.co.za** and join the Struik Nature Club
for updates, news, events and special offers

First published 2008
5 7 9 10 8 6 4

Publishing manager: Pippa Parker
Managing editor: Helen de Villiers
Editor: Emily Bowles
Design director: Janice Evans
Designer: Martin Endemann
Proofreader: Glynne Newlands

Reproduction by Hirt & Carter Cape (Pty) Ltd
Printed and bound by Craft Print Pte Ltd, Singapore

ISBN 978 1 77007 157 5

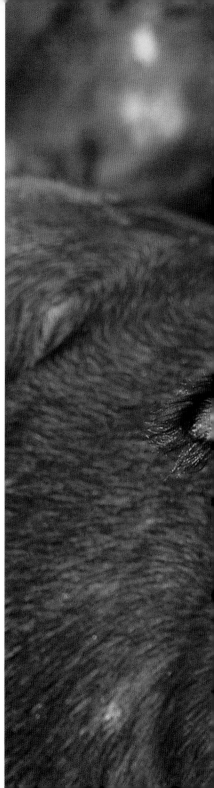

Contents

Page 1: An elephant calf enjoys a mud bath.
Pages 2–3: A young leopard photographed in the Sabie Sands Private Game Reserve, South Africa.
Page 5: African buffalo occur in large numbers, but have decreased in many areas as a result of both hunting and disease.
Left: In the Masai Mara National Reserve, Kenya, an adult male lion keeps a watchful eye on the camera.

Acknowledgements

A special thank you to the management and staff at all the places that I have been privileged enough to visit. Africa truly offers the best when it comes to destinations and friendly, efficient people in the tourism industry. I extend my thanks to them all, and my admiration for their contributions to conservation. Below I mention some of the organisations that have assisted me over the years.

Conservation Corporation has numerous captivating destinations throughout southern Africa and Zanzibar. Desert and Delta have always been helpful and supportive and their destinations offer good photographic opportunities. Kwando in Botswana is truly unforgettable and offers excellent game viewing. The Kruger National Park is probably one of the best known wildlife destinations in the world, where a tremendous diversity of wildlife can be observed. The luxurious MalaMala Game Reserve supports a great variety of animals and is situated adjacent to the Kruger National Park. Mokuti Lodge in Namibia, on the eastern border of the magnificent Etosha National Park, offers superb accommodation and exceptional game viewing in the dry months. Orient-Express have some wonderful destinations that are a delight to visit. Okonjima Game Reserve lies nestled in the unspoilt beauty of the Omboroko Mountains in Namibia. Big cats are almost always seen here. The Pilanesberg National Park in South Africa is close to Johannesburg, with the added attraction of Sun City nearby. Wilderness Safaris offer a wide range of lodges that provide wonderful African safaris in unspoiled, natural habitats. The Waterberg, situated in the far north of South Africa, is really magnificent and one of the younger 'Big Five' areas. Many of the locations in Kenya and Tanzania are also excellent for wildlife viewing. I wish to thank William Taylor for all the years of friendship and involvement with my projects. Most of the texts in this book are extracts from our highly successful book *Africa's Big Five*, which represents the combined efforts of William Taylor, Richard du Toit and myself.

The people at Struik Publishers have, as always, been a joy to work with. Thank you to all of those mentioned on the imprint page, as well as the rest of the team in Cape Town and Johannesburg.

GERALD HINDE
Johannesburg 2008

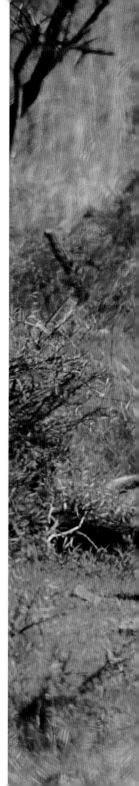

Right: A white rhinoceros with her calf in the Pilanesberg National Park, South Africa.

Introduction

AFRICA IS RENOWED FOR THE DIVERSITY OF ITS WILDLIFE, but it is the large mammals that command the most attention. The traditional Big Five – lion, leopard, elephant, rhino and buffalo – capture the spirit of the African bush and embody the legends of those early explorers and hunters who raised the status of these creatures above all others. The Big Five are the dominant animals of the grassland plains and deciduous woodlands that stretch across much of the subcontinent and, wherever they occur, they are the masters of their domain.

The term 'Big Five' probably originated in the early 1800s as a result of the increasing popularity of sport hunting. These were considered to be the most dangerous animals to deal with when confronted on foot, and the ones most capable of killing a human, so it was natural that they would become highly sought-after trophies for sport hunters venturing into the largely unknown 'dark continent'. These pioneer hunters left a legacy of adventure stories that romanticised their endeavours, but they

Left: This elephant and calf show signs of excitement as they approach the Chobe River in Botswana.

were also among the first Europeans to learn of the hunting practices and rituals of many African tribes. The most famous traditional hunt of all was conducted by the Maasai of Kenya, whose young warriors would go out to kill a lion armed only with a spear. This was a test of manhood and the warrior who killed the lion was entitled to wear its mane for the rest of his life. Ironically, the Maasai are the only African pastoral tribe still living with their cattle in the heart of lion country.

Nowadays, the majority of 'hunters' are armed with cameras, and the photographic safari has become a significant revenue earner for many African nations. But one thing has not changed: the Big Five are still the target of the 'hunt' and tourists are often willing to pay large sums to ensure that they 'bag' them all.

One thing the Big Five have in common is their affinity for the camera. Each, in its own way, offers the photographer the opportunity to document its unique characteristics and habits. Whether you are watching the seemingly studied indifference of a pride of resting lions or the edgy restlessness of buffalo heading for water, there is no end to the amount of time that can be spent observing Africa's giants and capturing their interactions with the other wildlife of the region, and even with one another.

Right: A lioness concentrates on stalking a herd of waterbuck on the banks of the Khwai River in Botswana.

Lion

LIONS HAVE AN EXTREMELY WIDE HABITAT TOLERANCE, being absent only from the interior of the Sahara Desert and the depths of Africa's tropical rainforests. Their optimum habitat is a combination of broken woodland and savanna, provided there is an adequate supply of suitable prey species, particularly wildebeest, buffalo, zebra and impala.

For all the magnificence of the male, lion society is strongly centred on the females and their relationships with one another. Lion social life is complex and variable, but the basic social unit, the pride, consists of a group of two or more closely related females and their cubs. The size and composition of an individual pride changes frequently, as subgroups spend time away, often to mate or raise cubs, before joining up again.

Hunting is a significant feature of pride life, and tends to be a collective effort aimed at maximising the chance of catching prey. Once a pride starts hunting in earnest, the lions maintain absolute silence and communicate via a series of subtle postures and movements. A practised pride operates as a single unit made up of

Left: The largest of Africa's big cats, the male lion is unmistakable. Throughout human history lions have been depicted as symbols of nobility.
Above: A lioness fights off the attentions of a young male.
Pages 16–17: Below the Oloololo Escarpment a pride of lions shares the open plains with a herd of elephants in Kenya's Masai Mara National Reserve.

individuals deeply in tune with one another's skills. But, once a kill is made, the males generally feed first, retiring only when they've had their fill. Feeding is a noisy affair with much slapping, growling, snarling and scratching taking place.

Within a pride, communication revolves around trying to avoid conflict – both with each other and with neighbouring prides. Long-distance communication includes scent marking and vocalisation, such as roaring, which advises other prides and nomadic males to keep out. However, facial expressions and body postures play an important role in closer communication. Lions have a uniform tawny body colour, with the exception of those parts used for communicating: the lips, nose, rims of the eyes, backs of the ears and tip of the tail are all black.

Above: A young lion defends an elephant carcass from Hooded Vultures.
Right: During the heat of the day lions often find elevated places to rest in order to catch any cool breezes.

Tactile communication includes sniffing, licking and head rubbing. The intensity of head rubbing is often a clue as to who are the more closely bonded members of the pride. Head rubbing functions mainly as a greeting, particularly for cubs, which greet by rubbing the top of their head against the chin of an adult. They will also arch their whole body and tail against the chest of an adult. Body posturing may be defensive or aggressive, and varies according to the degree of threat, but defence can turn to attack in a split second, leaving little time to distinguish between the two!

Left and above: Lionesses often show aggression towards younger members of the pride so as to establish their dominance.

Opposite: Lions are opportunists and will kill larger prey, such as this young hippo, when the opportunity arises.
Above: Lion cubs climb on top of an elephant carcass found lying alongside water.
Pages 24–25: Lion cubs are very active and playful during the cooler mornings and evenings; their antics provide tourists with hours of enjoyment.

Above and opposite: An elastic retractor ligament automatically withdraws the lion's claws when they are not in use. To extend the claws, the flexor muscles contract against the action of this ligament.

Pages 28–29: Lions and crocodiles are formidable enemies. Crocodiles have the advantage in water, but on land lions have been known to attack and kill large Nile crocodiles.

Left: Pride members reinforce their bonds by grooming one another.
Above: With his magnificent mane and imposing size, a healthy
male lion is an impressive sight.

Pages 32–33: In the cooler early morning hours, members of a lion pride frolic at a waterhole in Etosha, before resting through the heat of the day.

Opposite: A lioness will regularly move her cubs from one den to another during their first six weeks, to prevent predators from detecting their scent. The cubs are extremely vulnerable and only about 50 per cent live to maturity. Lion cub births are usually synchronised within a pride, which allows females to share their mothering duties.

Top and above: Play facilitates bonding within the pride and helps youngsters to acquire hunting skills.

Above: Once incoming male lions establish themselves as dominant in a territory that coincides with a pride (or prides) of females, they will kill any cubs that do not share their genetic material. This causes the lionesses to come into oestrus, and gives the new males an opportunity to perpetuate their own genes. The territorial males then protect the pride, and defend their cubs from other males.

Opposite: Lionesses abandon the pride to give birth, often moving some distance from their core range to do so.

Opposite and above: These lions had killed a buffalo calf earlier in the morning and had nearly finished eating the meat when a lone young elephant approached the Chobe River. In spite of her full stomach, the lead lioness immediately recognised an opportunity for an easy kill and took it. Lions in this area are renowned for their prowess at elephant hunting.

Elephant

ELEPHANTS ONCE OCCURRED THROUGHOUT AFRICA, but a combination of human settlement, ivory poaching and clearing of land for agriculture has greatly reduced their range and they now persist mostly in protected areas.

Elephants can live in any habitat that supplies them with sufficient food and water. They are found from the rainforests of West Africa to the subdesert of Namibia's kaokoveld and almost everywhere in between these two extremes: swamps, floodplains, highlands and montane forests, grasslands, arid scrub savanna and all types of woodland. Ideal elephant habitat contains a mixture of browse and graze where a variety of herbaceous, woody and grassy plants grow, and where there is enough shade and abundant water.

Elephants have the capacity to shape and change the environment in which they live. In their search for food, they break off branches and push over trees, dig holes in riverbeds that open up new waterholes, and their mud bathing and wallowing creates temporary pans that seasonally fill with water.

The seeds of some forest plants will not germinate unless they have passed through an elephant's digestive system, and the seeds of many grasses and savanna trees have

Left: Two playful young elephant bulls test each other's strength.
Above: In the dry winter months thousands of elephants congregate at the perennial Chobe River in Botswana.

far higher germination success if they are scarified in the gut of an elephant. In the course of its wanderings, the elephant moves these seeds from place to place, dispersing them as well as depositing them in a nutrient-rich pile of ready-made compost.

With their great strength and size, elephants must ingest huge amounts of food to meet the energy demands placed on them, and they can spend 16 hours of every day foraging and eating. Their digestive systems are relatively inefficient and, as a result, elephants take in some 150 to 200 kilograms of fresh food a day, while expelling up to 155 kilograms daily. They are able to utilise up to 90 per cent of available plant species, which facilitates the consumption of such a large volume. Food is picked or plucked from trees or shrubs, pulled down from trees up to six metres above the ground, pulled out of the ground, roots and all, or dug up from under the earth.

Using their trunk, tusks and feet in a highly coordinated fashion, elephants can manipulate anything from a full-grown tree to a tiny marula berry lying in long grass.

Elephants drink over 100 litres a day, but they also enjoy being in and around water. At muddy waterholes they roll in the mud or spray and slap it on themselves, often kicking with their legs to churn the mud into a good, sticky consistency. When well plastered they emerge from their bath and throw dust on themselves, concluding their ablutions by rubbing against trees or rocks.

Elephants have a complex social system – in reality, two systems existing alongside each other: male society and female society. The basic unit of an elephant herd is a mature cow, known as the matriarch, and her female offspring and relatives. This family group is closely bonded and may consist of as few as two or as many as 30 individuals. Adult males lead a bachelor existence in the company of other bulls, pairing up with females to mate.

Family groups have a connection to bigger kinship groups, the next level of elephant society, and these have connections to the more distantly related clans.

Pages 42–43: Elephants can live in any habitat that supplies them with sufficient food and water.
Right: Elephants love water. Their massive trunks are able to draw around four litres of water at a time, to be used for drinking or bathing.

Clans occupy the same range, and animals within that range, including lone bulls and those in bachelor herds, make up a sub-population.

Communication is an important facet of elephant life. These highly intelligent animals have a wide repertoire of sounds that not only express emotions but are undoubtedly specific to an individual, like a human voice. Obvious vocalisations include rumbling, trumpeting, squealing and screaming; elephants also make sounds that can carry over distances of more than two kilometres, but are inaudible to the human ear.

Their range of non-vocal communications includes postures and body movements that send specific messages to the watcher. Threat displays include 'standing tall' with ears spread on either side of the head, head shaking, and swishing the trunk forward accompanied by a blast of air or a loud trumpet. A charge is usually preceded by rocking backwards and forwards with one foreleg extended. Subtle changes in posture occur constantly and are used to communicate dominance or submission within the herd. Touch is so much a part of elephant life that even the casual observer can understand its role as a means of communication.

Elephants are very long-lived, with a lifespan of 60–70 years and, as such, have time to accumulate experience and knowledge. Like us, they have a long childhood in which to learn about their society and surroundings. They have tantrums when they are weaned, test the bounds of society and require discipline as they become rebellious teenagers and go through puberty, after which they gain independence, but still maintain close ties with family. Passing through maturity, they become aged and eventually die. To some observers, they even show an awareness of their own mortality, and their displays of emotion indicate the presence of conscious thought.

Left: A young elephant is always carefully tended by its mother, and any panicked squeals will bring her, and other members of the herd, to the rescue.

Above and right: A fusion of nose and upper lip, the versatile trunk is used for a range of tasks, from sucking up water and pushing over trees to delicately picking up marula berries.

Pages 50–51: During a late winter afternoon elephants congregate on the banks of the Chobe River in Botswana.
Below and opposite: An elephant's trunk serves many purposes such as squirting water and throwing up sand to achieve a dust bath, both of which help to rid the body of annoying insects.
Pages 54–55: Tusk size is genetically determined and age dependent but, on average, a 60-year-old bull carries 61 kg of ivory on either side of his trunk. Here, two mature bulls engage with each other as they cool off in a dam of water.

Above: A lioness watches as a family of elephants passes by. The elephant calf enjoys the protection of the mother, so would be reasonably safe from potential attack by the lioness.
Opposite: When alarmed or threatened, an elephant will not hesitate to charge.

Opposite and above: Two elephants in Etosha display a dramatic difference in colouring. The one on the left has just left a waterhole and is coated in dark mud, while the animal on the right is covered in white mud.

Above and opposite: Females first conceive at 10 to 12 years of age and thereafter give birth to a single calf every four to nine years. The gestation period is 22 months. A newborn weighs about 120 kg and stands 85 cm at the shoulder. Elephant herds are extremely protective of calves. **Pages 62–63:** The activities of elephants shape their environment; their mud bathing and wallowing even create temporary pans that fill with water.

Above: A family group of desert elephants makes its long journey to water.

Opposite: Addo Elephant National Park in South Africa has a thriving elephant population.

Pages 66–67: Clouds gather over Botswana's Savuti Reserve. 'Short rains' in November are followed by heavier, more sustained rainfall in February and March.

Leopard

LEOPARDS OCCUR THROUGHOUT AFRICA, except for the extreme interiors of the Sahara, Kalahari and Namib deserts. They are found in the depths of the rainforests, in arid regions and everywhere in between, even on the outskirts of villages and towns.

The leopard has a reputation for being a fearsome predator. It takes a variety of prey species, including antelope, hyrax (dassie), porcupine, mongoose, monkey, warthog, lizard, scrub hare and birds. The leopard's success as a hunter is largely due to its ability to adapt to its environment and to carve a niche for itself wherever it lives. An animal of supreme athleticism – powerful, fast, silent and well-armed in tooth and claw – it can take prey from the size of a mouse to an antelope many times bigger than itself. Furthermore, its physical attributes are complemented by an uncanny mental agility; leopards show great aptitude for learning the everyday business of hunting, as well as infinite patience during the hunt.

Although leopards often hunt during daylight hours, it is at night that they are at their most efficient, using a combination of sight, sound and smell to detect and catch prey.

Left and above: The background colour of a leopard's coat varies depending on its habitat. Generally, those that inhabit drier areas tend to have a lighter background colour, while animals in more heavily vegetated regions tend towards a richer gold.

Lions tend to rely mostly on hearing and cheetahs on eyesight, but the leopard uses a combination of senses when hunting.

Leopards lead an essentially solitary life, but this does not mean they have an uncomplicated social structure. Male and female leopards are both strongly territorial, and mark their territories regularly, with males doing more marking than females. Important and long-lasting territorial marks are made with scent, by spraying urine, leaving droppings, rubbing the scent glands on their cheeks onto trees or bushes, or by scraping the ground with their back legs.

Vocalising is another way of staking a territory. The leopard's call sounds like a saw rasping through dry wood; it is a series of deep, closely spaced grunts with what sounds like a sharp inhalation between each one. The call advertises a leopard's presence in an area and different leopards probably know one another's calls. Because leopards are hard to see under normal circumstances, this wonderful, mysterious sound is often the only memory of a leopard that visitors to the bush will take home with them.

The relationship between leopard and man has often been a troubled one. Sheep, goats, young cattle, poultry and domestic pets all fit into the leopard's ideal prey size, making contact and conflict between man and leopard inevitable.

There are estimated to be between 200 000 and 700 000 leopards in Africa, with many pockets of viable populations. The difficulty of seeing leopards in their natural habitat may have lent credence to the claim that it was in danger of extinction, but it is by far Africa's most successful big cat. If the existing populations are properly managed and protected, leopards should be around for many more generations of animal lovers to observe in the wild.

Pages 70–71: Leopards are resilient and have a very wide habitat tolerance. They can even exist, although in reduced densities, close to large human populations.
Right: When leopard cubs are approximately six months old, their mother begins to act aggressively towards them. Conflict escalates until she finally deserts her cubs and (at about 18 months) they become fully independent.

Left: A leopard's gestation period is 100 to 112 days, after which two cubs are usually born. They are blind at birth and open their eyes after 6 to 10 days.

Above: Male leopards measure 1.6 to 2.3 m from the nose to the tip of the tail, stand 60 to 80 cm at the shoulder and and weigh 31 to 65 kg.

Above: A leopard takes cover under a tree root as it stalks its victim. Throughout their range leopards take a staggering array of prey species. In Africa they tend to concentrate on the most abundant ungulates weighing between 20 and 80 kg.

Opposite: A young male leopard displays his disapproval at the photographer's approach.

Pages 78–79: A male leopard sets off to patrol his territory in the late afternoon.

Left and above: The Sabie Sands Private Game Reserve is renowned for its leopard viewing. These leopards are habituated to human observers and are therefore more relaxed.

Above: Leopards are expert climbers from a young age, which helps them to escape from the threat of being killed by lions and other dangerous predatory animals.

Right: Although it has disappeared in some areas and is greatly reduced in others, the leopard is not threatened within its African range.

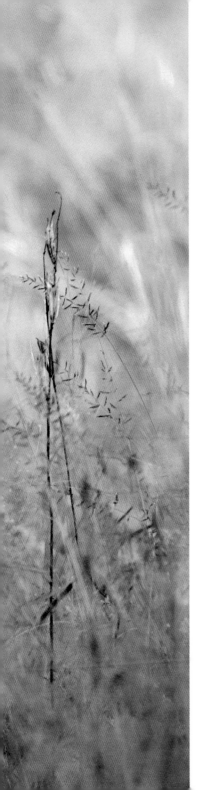

Left: The leopard's success is due to its ability to adapt to its environment and to carve a niche for itself across a variety of habitats.
Above: The leopard is a stocky, powerfully built spotted cat that is athletic and highly adaptable. It can take prey from the size of a mouse to an antelope many times bigger than itself.

Top: A leopard and her 22–month–old daughter move towards a thicket where she has stashed an impala carcass. Although already independent, the daughter has been accepted back for a day to feed off the carcass.
Above: With youthful inquisitiveness, a leopard cub peers curiously at the camera.
Opposite: Young warthogs are among the leopard's favourite prey, but the adults protect their offspring fiercely, so the piglets are not easily caught.

Pages 88-89: Leopards can be identified by the spot patterns on their faces. During his nine months of research at MalaMala Game Reserve, the photographer made detailed identity drawings of the leopards in the area, eventually distinguishing over 40 individuals.

Left: Caching prey in trees is key to this cat's remarkable ability to survive in areas where it competes with more powerful predators.

Above: From an early age, cubs show an innate skill in stalking and pouncing on prey.

Pages 92-93: Leopards are consumate stalk-and-ambush hunters, approaching prey as closely as possible before the final rush. The ultimate opportunists, these cats often kill young ungulates, like this duiker calf.

Pages 94–95: Leopards will drink surface water when available, but are not dependent on it.

Opposite: Most activity takes place on the ground but leopards are also capable climbers and swimmers.

Above: If they are under pressure from humans, leopards generally hunt at night. However, in areas where lions and hyaenas are nocturnally active, they are more likely to hunt by day.

Rhino

THERE ARE TWO SUBSPECIES OF RHINOCEROS IN AFRICA – the white or square-lipped, and the black or hook-lipped – but habitat preferences tend to keep them apart and they are seldom seem together. The white rhino grazes on open grassy plains and is often seen feeding, with its head angled towards the ground, while the black rhino browses in dense thickets where it feeds on trees, shrubs and herbaceous plants.

The rhino's large size, thick grey skin, short columnar legs and the prominent horns on the front of the face make it unmistakable. The main physical differences between the subspecies are that the white rhino is larger, with a wide, square lip, long head and straight-backed appearance, while the smaller black rhino has a hooked, pointed top lip, short, rounded head and hollow-backed appearance. The behaviour of calves is another indicator of species; the white rhino calf normally runs ahead of its mother and the black rhino calf runs behind her.

A rhino feeds and rests in alternate bouts throughout the day and night. Rhinos sleep soundly, usually during the hotter parts of the day.

Left: Historically, black rhino occurred throughout Africa south of the Sahara. Today they exist only in isolated populations in South Africa, Zimbabwe, Namibia, the Central African Republic, Cameroon, Tanzania and Kenya.
Above: The white rhino was in danger of extinction at the turn of the century. This animal's comeback is one of conservation's greatest success stories.

Black rhinos prefer areas with low shrubs and trees where they can feed and shelter from the heat. They occur in forest, woodland, scrub savanna and even open grassland if cover thickets are nearby. They need water for drinking and are seldom found more than 15 kilometres from a water source. Their prehensile, hooked upper lip is specially adapted for browsing, and these rhinos are very specific as to the size and type of shrubs on which they feed, favouring woody plants, acacia species and sickle bushes of less than a metre high.

White rhinos are purely grazers and take in huge quantities of grass, preferring dense short green growth which they crop with their wide, square lips. They are also dependent on water and usually drink twice a day, but have been known to go up to four days without drinking.

Rhinos are habitual wallowers and enjoy a good mud bath, especially in a drying pool where the mud is thick and sticky. Mud helps to cool the body by holding moisture against the skin, and it also helps to prevent insects from biting and irritating their skin. Both species, but especially white rhinos, form very marked trails that criss-cross their home ranges, leading from watering points to feeding and resting areas.

In general, rhinos tend to be solitary, although white rhinos seem to be more social than black rhinos. Both species can be semi-social, especially when younger, and it is rare to see rhino females or youngsters alone; the usual grouping is a female with her most recent calf. Newly independent youngsters may associate in same- or even mixed-sex groups of two to five animals. Dominant males occupy exclusive territories, but

Pages 100–101: The southern population of white rhino was slaughtered to within a hair's breadth of extinction, with as few as 50 individuals remaining in northern Natal. A handful of conservationists captured and translocated them and by 1970 this pocket of survivors had been carefully nurtured to over 2 000 animals.
Right: After conception, gestation lasts 15 months, and a single calf weighing about 45 kg is born. Here, a black rhino and calf browse on the open plains before retiring to the thickets.

tolerate the presence of subordinate males. A bull will even tolerate another dominant male within his territory, particularly a neighbour, as long as the visiting individual acts submissively. This arrangement is necessary because those individuals with no access to water must have a right of passage through a neighbouring territory to drink. Aggression is rare and most disputes are amicably settled, but in areas where territories are hotly contested, rhino fights can be protracted, bloody affairs, sometimes proving fatal for one or both combatants.

Rhinos make a wide range of sounds and can be very vocal. Both species have similar repertoires, and the most common sound is a puffing snort, rather like a loud inhaling and exhaling with a slight whistle to it. A variety of grunts, groans and snarls can be heard during normal interactions between individuals.

The black rhino earns its position as one of Africa's most dangerous animals through an inquisitive, irritable, aggressive and fearless nature, backed up by a 'charge first, ask questions later' attitude. During the filming of a Big Five documentary in the Pilanesberg National Park, the photographer spent a lot of time up trees or behind rocks whenever a black rhino was encountered. During six weeks of filming black rhinos, charges were frequent. In contrast, although white rhinos are the second-biggest land mammals on the planet, they are a lot more docile than their cousins.

Left: The rhino depends on water, both for drinking and for wallowing. Indeed, a bull will allow a neighbouring male to have access to water via his territory, provided the visitor acts submissively.

Left: Battles between white rhino are rarely serious. Only occasionally will severe or fatal wounds occur.
Above: A black rhino and a buffalo have a stand-off at a waterhole. Such stand-offs seldom lead to aggressive behaviour, but until a few mature elephant bulls were introduced into the elephant population at Pilanesberg National Park, young male elephants were found to be attacking and killing black rhino.
Pages 108 and 109: Although populations of black rhino are safe in some regions, this is still a highly endangered species. Black rhino populations in the Etosha Conservancy in Namibia have grown substantially.

Above: When in danger, a white rhino calf runs ahead of its mother in a high-kicking, bouncy gallop. By contrast, the black rhino calf follows its mother.
Right: Reintroduced populations of white rhino are thriving in the Waterberg, South Africa.

Opposite: A black rhino boasts a fine set of horns. The two prominent horns are composed of matted, hair-like filaments.

Above: Notoriously bad-tempered, the black rhino has not enjoyed good relations with humans. During a six-week period at Pilanesberg National Park, black rhinos charged the photographer on many occasions.

Pages 114–115: The black rhino is one of Africa's most dangerous animals, and is considered more aggressive than the white rhino. It is quick to charge if something makes it feel uncertain.

Left: Both species of rhino are generally solitary. White rhino, in particular, form marked trails, leading from watering points to resting areas.

Above: A rare moment of tenderness between a white rhino mother and her calf.

Above: A black rhino scratches an itch on a termite mound. Individuals will rub themselves against tree stumps, mounds or any other suitable object.

Opposite: A good example of the prehensile or hooked upper lip of a black rhino, which is specifically adapted for browsing. By contrast, the white rhino has a square lip that's suited to grazing.

Pages 120–121: Rhino populations appear to be stable at the moment, but authorities and conservation groups must remain vigilant so that they can respond quickly to outbreaks of poaching and other threats.

Buffalo

THE AFRICAN BUFFALO HAS A VERY WIDE sub-Saharan distribution and is one of the most successful herbivores on the continent. It is massive and thickset, with short, sturdy legs, a broad head, and ears that hang below its horns. Although both sexes carry horns, males have a large shield, called a boss, that develops at the top of their skull where the horns meet, while females have shorter, thinner horns and lack the massive development across the forehead.

Buffalo show a preference for habitat that provides plenty of food grasses and water, as well as shade from the midday sun. They inhabit savanna, swampy areas and montane forest, although here they will leave cover to graze in the clearing. They can even occupy more closed forest habitats and arid zones, provided that rivers or permanent waterholes are available.

Buffalo are predominantly grazers, subsisting on tall, coarse grasses, although some browsing is done in marginal habitats or when rains have been poor. They utilise natural salt licks but will also lick termite mounds, or even the mud off fellow herd members, to obtain salts. They are water-dependent and usually drink morning and evening.

Left: The African buffalo has a well-known symbiotic relationship with the Yellow-billed Oxpecker. The bird gets a regular supply of food, such as ticks, while the buffalo gets relief from parasites. In addition, when alarmed, the bird will hiss, helping to warn its host of impending danger.
Above: Buffalo and elephant gather at a waterhole.

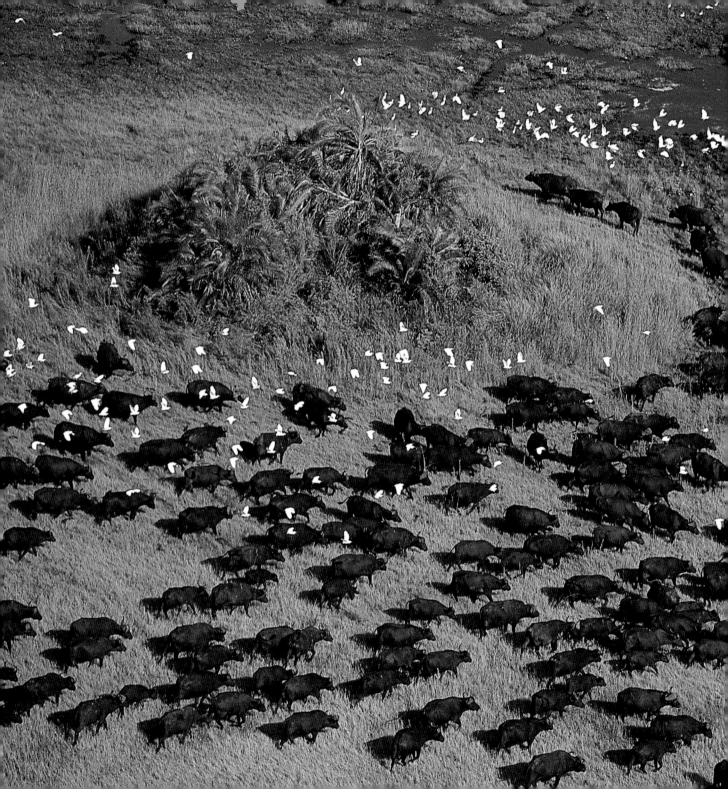

In parts of Africa, particularly along the richly grassed floodplains of the great rivers, buffalo travel in herds of up to 2 500 animals, but in mixed woodland and bushveld areas herds seldom number more than about 600. Large herds of buffalo are the most important bulk grazers on the African plains, removing the long, coarse grasses to expose new shoots for more specific grazers, such as zebra and wildebeest.

It was once assumed that buffalo society is matriarchal, but actually the prime reproductive bulls are dominant. However, it is not these dominant males who lead the herd to pasture and water, but rather 'pathfinder' animals, who take the lead in turns. The rest of the herd consists of subgroups, or clans, of related cows and their offspring from the last three years, each group being attended by a number of subadult or adult males.

Herds have clearly defined home ranges. Strangers are not tolerated, and those that try to join the herd often have such an unpleasant time that they are forced to leave. The main herd may split into smaller groups toward the end of the rainy season, but when the mating season begins all the buffalo in a particular range come together. A herd that is stationary and grazing tends to spread out, with each clan remaining together. When resting, clans lie down in tight groups.

When buffalo move long distances they usually do so at night, when it is cooler. Feeding takes place in the early morning and late afternoon. When the weather is cooler, the morning feeding session can last until midday. After feeding, the herd moves to a spot where the animals can lie down and ruminate, usually in the open or under shady trees or, if it is very hot and they are being bothered by biting flies, in thick bush.

Buffalo drink at least once a day, an activity that generates great excitement. When moving towards water, they utter a special call that is not heard at any other time. A buffalo herd is seldom silent; vocalisation plays a big part in keeping the herd together and there are specific calls for different activities. There is also much posturing to establish dominance and maintain order.

Pages 124–125: The Okavango Delta in Botswana has a substantial African buffalo population, with herds of over 1 000 individuals.
Right: After a good wallow, this African buffalo bull uses a tree stump as a scratching post to remove parasites trapped in the drying mud.

Pages 128–129: African buffalo are the most important bulk grazers on the plains. They remove the coarser grasses, which exposes finer shoots for specific grazers, such as zebra and wildebeest.

Opposite and above: A herd drinks in the early evening, and then travels back to the feeding grounds. This often involves moving through dangerous country, where bunching together tightly and staying alert helps to discourage lions from attacking.

Pages 132–133: When moving towards water, buffalo utter a special call, a long drawn-out *maaaaa* that spreads through the herd. As they get closer, excitement builds until the animals begin to trot and then gallop down to the water, walking in up to their knees.

Opposite: The savanna buffalo, the larger of the two subspecies of African buffalo, is particularly massive and thickset, carrying its heavy body on short, powerful legs. Males usually weigh around 700 kg, but may reach as much as 900 kg.
Above: Buffalo often lie in muddy pools during the heat of the day.

Above: As buffalo move through grass, their hooves disturb insects, which provides a windfall for Cattle Egrets.

Opposite: Members of a large herd move across the floodplains of the Chobe River in Botswana.

Above and right: Herds of African buffalo come down to drink in the late afternoon.

Page 140: The buffalo seems to have a relatively poor ability to regulate its body temperature, but mud wallowing and resting in shaded areas help prevent overheating.

Page 141: Both sexes carry horns. Males, such as this individual, have a large shield, called a boss, which develops on the top of the skull where the two horns meet; females have shorter, thinner horns with no massive development on the forehead.

Opposite: A large African buffalo bull in his prime stares out at the camera from among the mopane branches. Many hunters rate African buffalo as the most dangerous of the Big Five and numerous stories corroborate this. Placid when undisturbed, buffalo become unpredictable if provoked.

Above: A herd of African buffalo leaves the Chobe River as dusk falls.

Page 144, top: Duba Plains in Botswana is home to a number of lion prides as well as large herds of buffalo, and the interaction between them has been well documented. Though the cats in this area are excellent buffalo hunters, the herds have evolved various strategies to fight off lion attacks, thereby limiting predation.

Page 144, bottom: A rare opportunity presents itself as three of the Big Five – elephant, lion and African buffalo – are captured in one frame.